I CAN HELP Clean Our Air

Viv Smith

W
FRANKLIN WATTS

NEW YORK • LONDON • SYDNEY

First published in 1999 by
Franklin Watts
96 Leonard Street
London EC2A 4RH

© Franklin Watts 1999

Franklin Watts Australia
14 Mars Road
Lane Cove
NSW 2006 Australia

Editor: Helen Lanz
Art Director: Robert Walster
Designer: Sally Boothroyd
Environmental consultant: John Baines
Commissioned photography: Steve Shott
Illustrations: Kim Woolley

Printed in Hong Kong

ISBN: 0 7496 3199 6
Dewey Decimal Number: 363.73
A CIP catalogue record for this book is
available from the British Library.

Picture credits
Cover: Steve Shott
Interior Pictures: Franklin Watts all Steve
Shott images; Friends of the Earth 9/Richard
White, 12/Anne Longbottom, 20/Lawrence
Bruce, 21 tr/Michael Flood; Still Pictures 8
tr/T De Salis, 15/Mark Edwards; Viv Smith
10. All other photographs by Steve Shott.

The Publishers would like to thank
St. Leonard's Primary School, Stafford for
their help and enthusiasm, especially Viv
Smith and Class 2S who feature in this
series.

Thank you also to Still Pictures for supplying
additional pictures for this book.

Contents

The air we breathe

Run around, skip and jump. Do you feel 'puffed out', or out-of-breath? When we run about, we have to breathe more quickly. But we need to breathe all the time to stay alive.

Running about makes us take deep breaths.

✂ HAVE A GO!

Push an empty bottle into a bowl of water. Watch what happens. What do you think was in the bottle to make the bubbles?

We breathe in the air around us. We cannot see the air when it is clean, but we can feel it when the wind blows.

! FASCINATING FACT!

The moon has no air of its own. Astronauts landing there have to take their own air supply with them.

Air is made up of a mixture of gases. The main ones are nitrogen and oxygen, with tiny amounts of other gases, including carbon dioxide.

We use the oxygen in the air. When we breathe in, oxygen is taken to all parts of our bodies through our blood.

● Nitrogen: ● Oxygen: ● Carbon dioxide, water vapour, and other gases

These balloons are filled with air. Air is made up of different gases. Nitrogen and oxygen are the main ones.

All living things need to breathe.

Our bodies do not use carbon dioxide. We get rid of this when we breathe out. This carbon dioxide is not wasted, though. Plants use carbon dioxide, along with sunlight, to make food.

A breath of fresh air

Have you ever heard anyone say, "It's like a breath of fresh air!"? It means that something is clean and refreshing. But exactly how fresh is the air we breathe?

 ## HAVE A GO!

Find out how clean the air is around you. Get some pieces of clean, white plastic, or some white saucers. Put a thin layer of petroleum jelly over the plastic or saucers. Then put these in different places, such as in the kitchen, in the garden, near where your family parks the car, if you have one. Leave them for a few days, then collect them up. Note down what you see.

Which one is the dirtiest? Can you think why? Do you think it makes any difference if you live in the town or country?

WATCH OUT!

Have an adult with you if you place your saucers near the car or near anything hot in the kitchen.

Tall chimneys send fumes high into the air.

Smoke and fumes from car exhausts, factory chimneys, houses, power stations and the engines of aircraft, ships and trains get into the air.

Dirty air causes problems for people, making it hard for some people to breathe. It also causes problems for the environment.

Many people think that air pollution is one reason why more and more people have asthma.

9

Burning problems

Many of the things we do every day pollute the air. We need energy to make our cars go, to give us electricity so that we can turn on lights and watch television, and to allow us to cook our food and cool our drinks.

To get this energy we burn fuels such as coal, oil and gas. But when we burn these fuels, they pollute the air.

LOOK BACK

Look back to pages 6 and 7 to see where some carbon dioxide comes from.

A lot of fuel has to be burned to light up these many street lights.

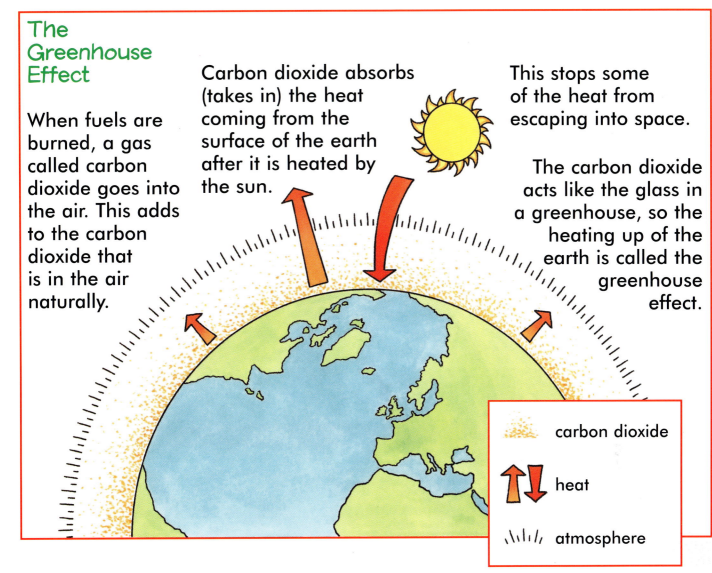

The Greenhouse Effect

When fuels are burned, a gas called carbon dioxide goes into the air. This adds to the carbon dioxide that is in the air naturally.

Carbon dioxide absorbs (takes in) the heat coming from the surface of the earth after it is heated by the sun.

This stops some of the heat from escaping into space.

The carbon dioxide acts like the glass in a greenhouse, so the heating up of the earth is called the greenhouse effect.

carbon dioxide

heat

atmosphere

We are adding more and more carbon dioxide to the earth's atmosphere. Because nature cannot absorb (take in) this extra carbon dioxide quickly enough, the earth is slowly warming up. This changes the temperature of the earth and changes our weather too. But there are things that we can do to help the earth to cope.

11

Acid rain

Smoke and exhaust fumes can also give us problems. The clouds above us are made up of tiny droplets of water in the air. When this water mixes with the smoke and fumes it forms an acid which falls as 'acid rain'.

Acid rain can kill plants and trees (right). It can pollute rivers and lakes and can kill the fish. It can also damage buildings.

The world is all connected. Pollution created in one country can cause acid rain in another.

FASCINATING FACT!

In the last 50 years, acid rain has caused more damage to stone buildings, such as churches, than damage caused by the weather over the last 500 years.

 HAVE A GO!

You can see for yourself the effect acid rain has on plants. Grow some cress seeds in two matching containers. Water one container with water from the tap. At the same time, water the other container with a mixture of water and lemon juice.

Do the seeds that you watered with lemon juice grow as well as the others?

! FASCINATING FACT!

Lemon juice is 1,000 times more acid than normal rain. In a place called Pitlochry, in Scotland, rain fell that was as acid as lemon juice.

The cress on the right has been watered normally. See how healthy it looks.

The cress on the left has been watered with lemon water. It has not grown very well.

13

Sun, sea and sunscreen

Do you like going to the seaside for your holiday? When you go to the beach, you probably put on sunscreen lotion. This helps to protect your skin from the sun's strong rays. If you stay in the sun for too long at one time without any protection, these rays can burn your skin.

Did you know that there's something else that also protects you from the sun's rays?

Different layers of gases go right up into space.

The earth is surrounded by layers of gases called the atmosphere. The layer closest to earth is where all the earth's weather takes place. The next layer above this has a gas in it called ozone.

80-500 km

50-80 km

15-50 km This layer contains ozone.

0-15 km Our weather takes place here.

The ozone layer acts as a screen against the sun's rays.

Ozone helps to protect us from the sun's harmful rays. But some of the things we use can harm the ozone layer. There are chemicals called CFCs that are used in refrigerators and air-conditioning systems. If these chemicals escape into the air they can damage the ozone layer.

There are simple things that we can do to help protect the ozone layer so that it can protect us. There are also things we can do to help to make a difference to the air we breathe and to keep it clean.

A smoke-free zone

No one likes a traffic jam. They are noisy, smelly and annoying. Yet, more and more places are being clogged up by traffic. And the more cars and lorries there are, the more pollution there is in the air we breathe.

So, what can we do to help keep our air clean?

Many cars today have 'catalytic converters'. These are things that make the fumes from cars cause less pollution.

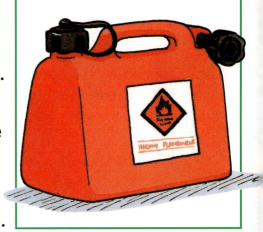

Find out what is being done in your local area to reduce air pollution.

Are there cycle lanes to encourage people to travel on their bicycles? Are cars banned from your town centre so that it's a cleaner and safer place to walk and shop? Are people encouraged to travel by bus by having cheaper fares and buses that run on time?

It's better to move as many people about in just one bus, than it is to have one or two people in lots of cars.

HAVE A GO!

Smoking is air pollution. Encourage your friends and family not to smoke by making a 'No Smoking' poster. Make sure it tells them how harmful smoking can be.

No smoking! This is a smoke free zone.

Clearing the air

All plants use carbon dioxide in the air to make them grow. As we breathe out carbon dioxide, plants help to reduce the amount of this gas in the air by 'breathing' it in.

So, the more trees and plants there are, the less carbon dioxide there is to keep the heat around the earth.

LOOK BACK

Look back to page 11 to see how too much carbon dioxide in the air makes the earth heat up.

Look around your local area. Are trees being cut down, or planted?

✂ HAVE A GO!

When you have finished eating your apple at lunch time, ask an adult to help you cut the core open to find the apple pips.

If the pips are ripe (they should be brown) collect them up carefully so that you can plant them.

Put them in a pot of soil and leave them on a window sill indoors. Don't forget to water them.

When your seedlings are big enough, you can plant them out into your garden at home or school.

Are you lucky enough to have a garden? Don't burn your garden waste – this will add to the air pollution. Instead, why not start a compost heap. If you don't have a garden, check to see if your local council has a composting centre. You can take your kitchen waste there.

! FASCINATING FACT!

Compost is a mixture of vegetable and plant waste. When it rots down, it is good for the soil. It helps plants grow.

19

Taking care of the air

We all use refrigerators and freezers to keep our food fresh and safe to eat.

When we get rid of our old, broken fridges, we can help protect the ozone layer by being very careful about how the fridge is thrown away (right).

Phone your council (who take away the rest of your rubbish) to ask them how to get rid of your fridge safely.

LOOK BACK

Look back to page 15 to see why refrigerators and freezers can harm the earth's atmosphere.

FASCINATING FACT!

Foam packaging used to be made using CFCs. This way of making packaging is now banned in Britain. Fast food restaurants once used it, but today most of them use recycled card and paper for their boxes, bags and napkins.

We can also help to keep the air clean by saving energy. Making electricity and using gas burns fuels. This produces the gas carbon dioxide which adds to the greenhouse effect. But there are some sources of energy that we can all use that don't pollute the air.

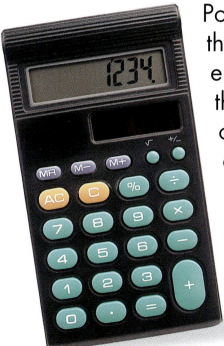

Power from the sun (solar energy) and the power of the wind are natural sources of

energy. Help hang out the washing, rather than put it in the tumble drier. Do you ever use a calculator? Why not use one that runs on solar energy instead of batteries?

The 3 Rs

The more things that are made in factories, the more air pollution is caused. Think carefully before you throw something away that you could use again or that someone else might want.

Reduce, re-use, recycle!

LOOK BACK

Many of the things we buy are made in factories. Look back to page 9 to see how factories can pollute the air.

FASCINATING FACT!

Over a quarter of the material used by factories that make packaging in Britain is recycled.

Look out for recycling signs like the ones below when you go shopping.

HAVE A GO!

REDUCE ...

... the amount of electricity you use – switch the television off when you leave an empty room

... the need for plastic bags – use boxes or a cloth bag for your shopping

... the number of car journeys you take – walk or cycle when you can

RE-USE ...

... envelopes – stick clean paper on the front so you can write a new address

... books – swap them for ones you haven't read

... clothes – pass your clothes on to your sisters and brothers when you have grown out of them

RECYCLE ...

... old newspapers – take them to the recycling centre

... tins and drink cans – take them to the recycling centre too

... glass bottles – you've guessed it, take these to the recycling centre at the same time

Put the list up somewhere that will remind everyone to use the 3 Rs. Now you're helping!

23

Make a difference

✂ HAVE A GO!

Play a game of 'domino-rally'. Set up the dominoes on end, just apart but not touching each other.

Tap the first domino gently. Watch what happens to all the other dominoes.

👀 LOOK BACK

Look back to pages 16, 17, 18, 19, 20, 21, 22, and 23 to see how we can help to clean our air.

The world and its systems of plants and animals, land, water and air is like the dominoes. If we spoil one of them, we can affect the others too. But if we look after one, this helps protect the other systems as well.

Sometimes it can seem that some problems are just too big for us to do anything about.

But there are many things that we can do to help protect our environment and to make the air cleaner.

Here's a reminder of some of the things we can do.

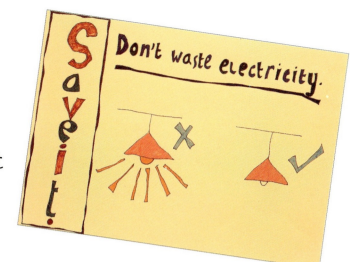

❀ Remember to turn off lights and the television when you don't need them. This means less fuel is burned, which means less pollution.

❀ If your journey is a short one, why not walk or cycle?

❀ Ask your mum or dad to have the car checked regularly to make sure it doesn't give out really bad fumes.

❀ Reduce, re-use or recycle your waste then there is less waste to get rid of.

If we help to do these little things, they can all add up to make a big difference!

More activities and facts

FASCINATING FACT!

Re-using and recycling materials can help keep the air clean. Some supermarkets have collection points for unwanted plastic bags. Making plastic bags out of recycled polythene produces less carbon dioxide than making new bags.

FASCINATING FACT!

Some bus operators now use City Diesel to run their buses. This causes less smell. It is also less likely to cause acid rain than other diesel fuels.

HAVE A GO!

If you go on a picnic, try not to use throwaway cups, plates and cutlery. They take a lot of energy to produce. Use ones which can be re-used – and then wash them up by hand!

LOOK BACK

Look back to pages 12 and 13 to find out about acid rain.

26

✂ HAVE A GO!

Go with an adult to your local DIY (Do It Yourself) store. Look for all the different types of masks that people use to breathe through when they don't want to breathe in fumes. Have you ever seen a cyclist or someone working using one of these masks?

✂ HAVE A GO!

Driving fast and stopping suddenly uses up a lot more fuel than driving at the same speed. It also makes the car give out more fumes. Ask your family and friends to drive smoothly and to keep to a slower speed.

👀 LOOK BACK

Look back to pages 10 and 11 to find out about carbon dioxide.

! FASCINATING FACT!

If you recycle 20 aluminium cans, you will save enough electricity to run your television for one hour.

alu can
recycling
CARING FOR THE ENVIRONMENT

Useful words

acid rain: rainfall that absorbs (takes in) the pollution from burning fuels like oil and coal. Acid rain can damage wildlife and buildings.

aluminium: a light metal used to make many things including drink cans, containers, cars, and even aeroplanes.

asthma: a condition where people have problems with breathing, especially if the air is dirty.

atmosphere: the air surrounding the earth.

CFCs: chlorofluorocarbons. Gases used in refrigerators and air-conditioning systems. They can damage the ozone layer.

council: a group of people voted for by others in a local area in order to look after that area. Councils arrange for our rubbish to be collected and recycling bins to be emptied.

energy: power that gives us the ability to light things, heat and cool things, and to drive things, such as machines.

environment: the air, land and water where plants, people and animals live.

exhaust: waste gases from the engines of cars and lorries.

fumes: smoke and gases which make the air dirty and unpleasant to breathe.

ozone: a gas found in the atmosphere. It helps to protect us from the sun's rays.

pollute: to make the land, air or water sources dirty.

recycle: to make something new out of something which has been used before.

reduce: to use less of the earth's resources. By buying fewer goods, we reduce the need to make new things.

waste: rubbish. Left over things that are no longer wanted.

Index